"Whispers of the Soul: A Journey Through Poetry"

David Fiori

BookLeaf Publishing

India | USA | UK

Presentation by *BookLeaf Publishing*

Web: www.bookleafpub.com

E-mail: info@bookleafpub.com

ISBN: 9789360945039

First edition 2024

Dedication

To my Fiancée, Monica Canul,

*In the tapestry of my life, you are the vibrant
thread that binds it all together. Your love and
unwavering support have been the guiding light
illuminating my path, even in the darkest of
times. With each step we take together, I am
reminded of the beauty of companionship and
the strength found in shared dreams.*

*This book is a testament to the depth of my love
for you and the gratitude I hold in my heart for
all that you are.*

With all my love,

David Fiori

ACKNOWLEDGEMENT

I am indebted to my readers, whose embrace of my words has filled my heart with warmth and purpose. Your connection to my poetry fuels my creativity and reminds me of the profound power of storytelling.

A special appreciation goes to my editor and publishing team, whose dedication and expertise have transformed my words into a tangible work of art. Your guidance and passion have been invaluable on this literary voyage.

Lastly, I offer my deepest thanks to the muses that whisper to me in the quiet moments, guiding my pen with their gentle touch. Without your ethereal presence, this book would remain but a dream unfulfilled.

PREFACE

"In crafting 'Whispers of the Soul,' I embarked on a deeply personal journey, seeking solace in the rhythm of words and the melody of emotions. Each poem emerged as a testament to my own experiences, a cathartic release of the joys and sorrows that have woven the tapestry of my life. Through this collection, I aspire to share not only my vulnerabilities but also the profound resilience that resides within us all. May these verses serve as a beacon of hope, guiding readers through their own tumultuous seas and reminding them of the beauty found in every whispered echo of the soul."

Rising Above

"Rising Above"

In the shadows, where darkness held sway,
A soul once lost in the depths of dismay,
Caught in the grip of addiction's sway,
Yearning for dawn to break the night away.

Through the haze of despair, a flicker of light,
A glimmer of hope amidst the endless night,
Courage found in the depths of the fight,
To rise from the ashes, to reclaim what's right.

With each step forward, a new path unfolds,
A journey of healing, where strength beholds,
The power within, a story retold,
Of resilience, of redemption, of a spirit bold.

So let the echoes of triumph resound,
As the chains of addiction are unbound,
For in the heart's darkest hour, true freedom is
found,
In the soul's ascent, where new beginnings
abound.

"Echoes of Absence"

In the twilight of adolescence, a son's world
fractures,
As the pillar of his existence crumbles,
Leaving behind shards of memories to piece
together,
In the caverns of his grieving heart.

The echo of his father's voice lingers,
In the rustle of autumn leaves,
In the quiet moments before dawn,
A reminder of the bond that transcends time.

With each passing day, the void deepens,
Yet, in the depths of despair, resilience blooms,
As the son learns to carry the legacy of his
father,
A torch to illuminate the path ahead.

Though the ache of loss may never fully subside,
In the tapestry of his life, his father's love
weaves,
Guiding him through the labyrinth of existence,
Until they reunite in the embrace of eternity's
embrace.

"Beneath the Neon Veil"

In the urban sprawl, where neon lights blaze,
I walk alone through the city's maze.
Lost in the crowd, but drowning in fear,
Yearning for someone to draw near.

In the glow of screens, I search for connection,
But find only shallow reflection.
Aching for love in a digital age,
Yet drowning in loneliness, trapped in a cage.

In the dead of night, when the streets are still,
I feel the void, an endless chill.
No one to hold, no one to hear,
Just the echo of my own silent tear.

The fear of dying alone grips me tight,
In this modern world, where connections feel
right.
But as the city hums with life's ceaseless drone,
I pray for solace, to not face death alone.

"Eclipse of the Unknown"

In shadows deep, where whispers roam,
There lies the realm we call our own.
In alleys dark and streets unnamed,
The unknown of life, forever unclaimed.

We dance upon a razor's edge,
Through realms of pain and dreams unsaid.
In every step, a gamble made,
As we navigate this masquerade.

Our hearts beat wild, our souls aflame,
In search of truths that bear no name.
We wander lost, yet unafraid,
Through the abyss where fears are laid.

In the chaos of the night,
We find our peace, our delight.
Embracing darkness, we defy,
The boundaries that confine our sky.

For in the unknown, we find our spark,
Igniting flames in shadows dark.
We'll carve our path, uncharted, bold,
In the mystery of life, we'll hold.

So let us revel in the unknown,
For in its depths, our seeds are sown.
With every breath, a new frontier,
In the edgy dance of what's unclear.

"Envy's Embrace"

In shadows deep, where envy thrives,
A sibling's heart with poison thrives.
Each glance a dagger, each word a wound,
In every crevice, bitterness is groomed.

From tender youth, a seed did sow,
A rivalry that refused to outgrow.
In the mirror's gaze, resentment blooms,
As jealousy consumes and entombs.

Yet beneath the surface, a tale untold,
Of love unspoken, of dreams withheld.
For envy masks a yearning deep,
To share the bond, to bridge the keep.

So let compassion quell the fire,
And empathy be the chord that inspires.
For in understanding, we find release,
From envy's grasp, we find our peace.

"Awakening of Bliss"

Like a dormant seed beneath winter's frost,
Joy stirs within, a feeling long lost.
Through veils of sorrow, it starts to rise,
A sunlit dawn in weary eyes.

With hesitant steps, I embrace the light,
As warmth of happiness melts the night.
A symphony of laughter, a dance of glee,
Resurrecting fragments of the me I used to be.

Memories cascade like gentle streams,
Awakening hopes, shattered dreams.
For in this moment, I am reborn,
In the tender embrace of joy, tattered hearts
adorn.

With newfound courage, I embrace the day,
Basking in the glow, come what may.
For in the depths of darkness, I found my light,
And in the echoes of joy, I take flight.

"Maze of Uncertainty"

In the labyrinth of existence, I wander lost,
Questions echo, dreams exhaust.
Each turn a twist of fate unknown,
In the haze of uncertainty, I'm thrown.

The roadmap of life, a cryptic maze,
With paths diverging in endless ways.
Confusion reigns, doubts cascade,
As clarity eludes, and fears pervade.

Yet amidst the chaos, a whisper persists,
A beacon of hope in the dense mist.
For in the heart's chambers, a truth resides,
That in the journey's trials, wisdom abides.

So I navigate this labyrinthine strife,
Embracing the uncertainty of life.
For in the confusion, I find my way,
In the dance of shadows, I learn to sway.

"Racing Thoughts"

In the silence of the night, my mind takes flight,
A whirlwind of thoughts, an endless plight.
Like a restless river, it rushes and roars,
Leaving me stranded on anxious shores.

Each heartbeat echoes a frantic drum,
As worries cascade, fears overcome.
A relentless storm in the depths within,
Tangled thoughts, a cacophony of din.

In the labyrinth of my mind, I seek reprieve,
But anxiety's grip, it refuses to leave.
Like a tangled web, it ensnares my soul,
Leaving me gasping, losing control.

Yet amidst the chaos, a glimmer of light,
A beacon of calm in the darkest night.
For in the stillness, I find my grace,
In acceptance of this frenzied race.

"Echoes of Worthlessness"

In a dingy apartment, dark and drear,
Two roommates dwell, consumed by fear.
Their dreams once soared, now lost in haze,
Trapped in a cycle, a hopeless maze.

One sits in silence, lost in thought,
The other, restless, feeling fraught.
Their presence lingers, heavy in the air,
Each suffocating in their own despair.

Their aspirations, like paper, crumpled and torn,
Forgotten desires, once brightly worn.
They've become strangers in their own abode,
Lost in the shadows of the life they've erode.

Bitter words exchanged, but no one hears,
Only echoes in the emptiness, their fears.
They're bound together, yet miles apart,
Their souls entwined, yet torn apart.

They know they must part, this toxic bond,
But fear grips tight, they're too far gone.
So they linger in limbo, drowning in sorrow,
Hoping for a better tomorrow.

Yet the truth remains, stark and clear,
They're worth more than the doubts they hear.
It's time to break free, to find their worth,
To leave behind the darkness, embrace rebirth.

So they gather their courage, amidst the strife,
And step into the unknown, reclaiming life.
For even in darkness, there's a flicker of light,
Guiding them forward, out of the night.

"Unleashed Radiance"

In the quiet hours before dawn's embrace,
A stirring within, a newfound grace.
A whisper of dreams, once tucked away,
Now dance in the soul, eager to sway.

A spark ignites, within the heart's deep well,
A symphony of possibilities, begins to swell.
The shadows of doubt, begin to fade,
As the brilliance of potential is displayed.

Each breath drawn in, with a newfound might,
Ignites the flames of a passionate flight.
The past's heavy chains, now fall away,
As the spirit ascends to meet the day.

With eyes alight, and spirit unbound,
The world's vast canvas, awaits unground.
No longer held back by fear or constraint,
But propelled forward, by dreams unfeigned.

In every step, a melody resounds,
As aspirations soar, to higher grounds.
The once dormant soul, now fully awake,
In the pursuit of purpose, no longer fake.

For in the realization of one's true self,
Lies the key to unlock life's wealth.
So let the world witness, this radiant glow,
As the journey of fulfillment continues to flow.

With each passing moment, a new height to
scale,
In the pursuit of dreams, we shall prevail.
So embrace the journey, with hearts aglow,
For the potential within, shall continue to grow.

"Unleashed Radiance" — a beacon bright,
Guiding the way, through day and night.
For in realizing one's full potential's gleam,
Lies the essence of life's wondrous dream.

"Embrace the Unknown"

In the silent chambers of my mind,
Whispers of doubt, unkind, unkind.
Fears lurking in shadows deep,
Where courage falters, and dreams sleep.

A labyrinth of worries, twists and turns,
Where hesitation ignites and confidence burns.
But amidst the darkness, a flicker of light,
A beacon of hope, burning bright.

With trembling hands, I grasp the thread,
Leading me from the depths of dread.
Step by step, I navigate the maze,
Confronting fears in myriad ways.

No longer content to cower and hide,
I face the demons, stride by stride.
For within this struggle, lies the key,
To unlock the shackles and set me free.

With each obstacle, I learn and grow,
Embracing the discomfort, letting it flow.
For in the heart of fear, lies the chance,
To find courage, to take a stance.

So I journey onward, through the unknown,
With resilience as my compass, I am not alone.
For in the pursuit of overcoming strife,
I discover the depths of my inner life.

"Embrace the Unknown" — a mantra to declare,
In the face of fear, I'll meet it there.
For within its grasp, lies the power to soar,
And unlock the gates to a life worth more.

"The Melody's Burden"

In the silent hum of the dawn's first light,
Where dreams are born and souls take flight,
There lies a world of melodies untold,
Where the brave and the bold dare to hold.

Through the alleys of uncertainty they roam,
In search of a place they can call home,
Their notes weave tales of joy and pain,
In the labyrinth of music's domain.

The road they tread is rugged and steep,
With promises to keep and dreams to reap,
Yet each chord they strike, each lyric penned,
Carries a weight that never seems to end.

For behind the glamour, beneath the fame,
Lurks a relentless beast, a relentless game,
Where success is a fleeting, elusive prize,
And failure's shadow looms in disguise.

They battle the critics, they fight the odds,
Their hearts bleeding on makeshift façades,
For every applause, a thousand doubts,
For every triumph, a hundred droughts.

Yet still they press on, against the tide,
With passion as their compass, and music as
their guide,
For in every note, in every line,
They find solace, they find divine.

So here's to the troubadours, the minstrels bold,
Whose stories are etched in melodies untold,
May their journey be blessed, their burdens
light,
As they navigate the darkness and embrace the
light.

"Pulse of the Spotlight"

In the trembling hush before the storm,
I stand alone, my spirit warm,
Heart pounding like a thunderous drum,
As anticipation grips each strum.

The stage awaits, a hungry beast,
Its hunger fueled by my release,
I step into its glaring light,
A gladiator in the night.

Adrenaline surges, a wild cascade,
As I step forth, unafraid,
Words ignite like sparks of flame,
In the theater of the untamed.

Eyes upon me, a thousand stares,
Their whispers humming in the air,
But in this moment, I am free,
Bound only by my poetry.

Each syllable, a lightning strike,
Each verse a battle, a righteous fight,
For in this space, I am reborn,
A phoenix rising from the scorn.

I dance upon the razor's edge,
Between ecstasy and the dredge,
My voice a weapon, sharp and keen,
In the symphony of the unseen.

And as the final stanza rings,
I feel the rush, the soaring wings,
For in this spotlight, I'm alive,
A poet conquering the dive.

So let the stage be my domain,
Where passion flows like pouring rain,
For in the glare of the roaring crowd,
I find my voice, fierce and proud.

"Flames of Revelation"

In innocence's embrace, I once did roam,
A world of wonder, a place called home,
But shadows lurked beneath the sun,
And innocence's reign was soon undone.

For I learned swiftly, at youth's tender stage,
That not all hearts beat on the same page,
Some wielded daggers, disguised as smiles,
Their intentions cloaked in deceptive guiles.

Betrayal's sting, a bitter pill to swallow,
As illusions shattered, leaving me hollow,
But from the ashes, a phoenix rose,
With newfound wisdom, I chose to impose.

I forged my path, with caution's grace,
Steering clear of those with venomous embrace,
For toxic souls, like flames, consume,
Leaving scars that linger, like a gloom.

With armor forged from lessons learned,
I stood resilient, my spirit unburned,
Distancing myself from the poisoned fray,
To bask in the light of a brighter day.

No longer bound by deceit's cruel snare,
I journey forth with vigilant care,
For in the crucible of deceit's cold gaze,
I found the strength to walk away.

"Mind's Battlefield"

In the chaos of the modern fray,
Where stress and worries hold sway,
Mental fortitude becomes our might,
In the relentless march through the night.

In the battlefield of the mind we stand,
Against the tides of fear, we expand,
For in this age of constant strife,
Our mental well-being is our life.

Amidst the clamor of daily grind,
Our sanity becomes refined,
For in the quiet of our soul's retreat,
We find the strength to face defeat.

In the echo chambers of our thoughts,
Anxiety's whispers become fraught,
But through self-care and self-compassion's
grace,
We find the courage to embrace.

To tend to the wounds that lie within,
To nurture the spirit, to let it begin,
For mental health is not a trend,
But a journey upon which we must depend.

So let us raise our voices high,
And break the silence, amplify,
The importance of mental care,
In times of adversity, we dare.

For in the depths of our darkest night,
It is our minds that lead the fight,
And through resilience, we shall prevail,
In the modern world's tempestuous gale.

"Embracing Euphoria"

In the crucible of self-discovery, I stand,
Embracing the echoes of a newfound land,
Where shadows fade and light prevails,
And courage dances in the veils.

No longer bound by doubts' cruel chains,
I rise, a phoenix from infernal flames,
For in the depths of self-reflection's gaze,
I found the strength to break free from the maze.

Every scar, a testament to resilience,
Every tear, a token of defiance,
For in the furnace of adversity's breath,
I forged a spirit, unyielding to death.

With every step, a symphony unfolds,
In the rhythm of the stories untold,
New adventures beckon, daring and bold,
As I walk paths of silver and gold.

The past, a canvas painted in hues of pain,
But now, I dance beneath the pouring rain,
With every heartbeat, a thunderous drum,
In the anthem of a life finally won.

So let the winds of change sweep me away,
To realms where dreams in technicolor play,
For in this moment, I am free,
In the edgy embrace of my destiny.

Unveiling Pride

In the quiet corners of my mind,
A whisper rises, soft and kind.
A voice that speaks of journeys trod,
Of battles fought, and doubts unshod.

Through trials vast and fears untamed,
I've journeyed forth, my path reclaimed.
With every step, a newfound stride,
A sense of self, no longer denied.

In the mirror's gaze, I now see clear,
The strength within, dispelling fear.
No longer bound by others' gaze,
I walk with pride, through life's maze.

For every stumble, every fall,
Was but a step towards standing tall.
Each scar a tale of resilience shown,
Inscribed upon this flesh and bone.

No longer shackled by past mistakes,
I rise above, my spirit awakes.
Embracing flaws, they make me whole,
A masterpiece of heart and soul.

So here I stand, with head held high,
A testament to resilience, I defy.
For I am proud, of who I've become,
A journey of self-love finally won.

"Earth's Splendor"

Title: Earth's Splendor

In the cradle of the cosmos, she reigns supreme,
Mother Earth, in her beauty, a timeless dream.
Her skin adorned with verdant greens and azure blues,
A masterpiece of nature, in every hue.

Mountains rise like guardians, reaching for the sky,
Their peaks crowned with snow, majestic and high.
Valleys lay nestled, in their gentle embrace,
Where rivers dance freely, with elegance and grace.

Forests stand proud, a cathedral of green,
Whispering secrets, in every rustling scene.
Their canopies a sanctuary for creatures small,
In harmony they dwell, in nature's grand hall.

Fields of gold stretch out, beneath the sun's warm glow,
A tapestry of life, in constant ebb and flow.

Beneath the waves, a world unseen yet
wondrous,
Where coral reefs flourish, in hues lustrous.

The desert sings its own song, of arid lands,
Where dunes shift and sway, in winds' gentle
hands.
Yet even in its harshness, beauty does abide,
In the quiet moments, where serenity resides.

Mother Earth, in her splendor, a sight to behold,
A treasure trove of wonders, both young and
old.
Let us cherish her gifts, with hearts open wide,
For in her embrace, true beauty resides.

" Melodies of Life"

In the rhythm of existence, music weaves its
thread,
A symphony of emotions, in every note
widespread.
From the gentle lullabies that cradle us to sleep,
To the anthems that stir our souls, running deep.

In melodies, we find solace, a refuge from life's
storm,
A language universal, in which hearts can
perform.
With each chord strummed and each lyric sung,
We find connection, where once we felt alone
and wrung.

In the silence, music speaks volumes, without a
word,
Expressing joys, sorrows, and everything in
between heard.
It paints pictures in our minds, evoking
memories so dear,
Transporting us through time, making the
present clear.

Through music, we celebrate, we mourn, we love,
It's a gift bestowed upon us, from the heavens above.
From the grandeur of orchestras to the simplicity of a song,
Its power knows no bounds, it's where we all belong.

So let us revel in its beauty, let it fill our souls with light,
For in music's embrace, we find our might.
A testament to the human spirit, a beacon in the night,
Music, the greatest gift, guiding us through life's flight.

"Soul's Embrace"

Beneath the azure canopy, bathed in golden hue,
The sun caresses my spirit, a warmth so true.
Its rays, like gentle fingers, touch my soul,
Awakening dormant dreams, making me whole.

In the embrace of sunlight, worries fade away,
As if kissed by heaven, in the light of day.
A symphony of warmth, a dance of light,
Filling me with joy, banishing the night.

Each beam a blessing, each ray a balm,
Healing wounds unseen, bringing calm.
I bask in its glow, in a tranquil trance,
Feeling the sun's embrace, in every glance.

With each passing moment, I'm renewed,
In the sun's loving gaze, I'm imbued.
It whispers secrets of the universe untold,
As I surrender to its warmth, my spirit bold.

Oh, how divine it feels, to be touched by the sun,
To feel its radiance, every battle won.
In its embrace, I find serenity and grace,
For the warmth of the sun is where I find my
place.

"Silent Echoes"

Since I was nineteen, a silent ache I bear,
A weight upon my heart, a burden I must bear.
For every day without you feels like a hollow
space,
A void within my soul, where memories
embrace.

I miss your laughter, your guidance, your gentle
touch,
Moments shared together, I miss them all so
much.
But silently I carry, this longing deep inside,
Holding onto memories, where love and pain
collide.

Each day I wake, your absence cuts like a knife,
Yet I keep it hidden, behind a stoic guise.
For words seem inadequate, to express this silent
grief,
So I keep it to myself, seeking no relief.

But oh, how I miss you, more than words can
say,
Every moment, every hour, every passing day.
The ache of your absence, a constant refrain,

Yet in my heart, your love forever will remain.

So I'll hold onto the memories, keep them close
and dear,
Treasures of a lifetime, to soothe my silent tears.
For though you're gone, your spirit lingers on,
In the quiet moments, in the breaking dawn.

And though I may never speak of the pain I feel
inside,
Know that you are missed, each day, each
moment, each tide.
For you were more than just a father, you were
my guiding light,
And I'll carry your love with me, through the
darkest night.

Each beam a blessing, each ray a balm,
Healing wounds unseen, bringing calm.
I bask in its glow, in a tranquil trance,
Feeling the sun's embrace, in every glance.